111
PERCEPTIONS
OF LIGHT

111 PERCEPTIONS OF LIGHT

A BOOK OF POETIC INSPIRATION
FOR THE SPIRITUAL PATH

Mattaeo Kleine

KLEINE PUBLISHING HOUSE

Editor: Michael Martin
Cover & Interior Design: JBookDesigns

ISBN: 979-8-9927022-1-7 Paperback
ISBN: 979-8-9927022-2-4 Hardcover
ISBN 979-8-9927022-0-0 eBook
PCN: 2025907540

Kleine Publishing House LLC
13575 58th Street North Suite 200
Clearwater, FL 33760

Dedicated to all who are discovering their spiritual nature in a physical reality. May your higher awareness lead you to the place where your soul belongs.

CONTENTS

ACKNOWLEDGMENTS

I would like to extend a word of sincere thanks to my angels, ancestors, and ascended masters. All who walk with me while existing in non-corporeal form. They have served as my dearest reminders, as when the journey requires one to walk alone, they never walk alone.

INTRODUCTION

You were born magnificent, and you leave
here divine, for all are but source energy
merely working its way back to itself.

CHAPTER 1

JOURNALS OF A SEER

Soul Speaks Light

When the energy expands,
new vibrations unfold,
showing me what my spirit
holds. It tells me subtle
secrets that make me aware
of the stories that must be
told. It uplifts my heart and
enlightens my mind, so
that I can sing new songs. It
prepares me to communicate
from my spirit and not the
tongue. With a still grace and
gratitude, I arise to speak
new truths. The source is
light, its energy ignites and
awakens the soul to its sooth.

I Am

I am an expression of all
things, as all things are an
expression of me. There are
no boundaries in which I can
be contained. Limitations
are not a product of me, for
I extend from the source
of all energy, as the source
extends through me. I am
undefinable by terminologies,
as there are no concepts in
which I can truly be, but for
a statement I proclaim as an
expression of me, in harmony
with all reflections of me.

I am.

As I Walk

As I take the hand of spirit, I
go beyond the physical scene.
I gain access to a place my
soul reveals to me. It shows
me reality, and my filters
wash away. I see a different
side of life and truth that
always stays: for my lifespan
is eternal, and this life is a
role I play. Death is but an
illusion. It gives an excuse
to walk away. Though I was
never meant to stay. I have
many things to do. How
do you measure a lifetime
when eternity is your truth?
I embrace the reality my
soul reveals to me. I let go of
life's illusions, and it set my
spirit free. I no longer walk
the path designed by society.
I took the hand of spirit.
Now, I walk in my destiny.

Universal Love

I align myself with the sound
of creation. The universe is
one with me. I transcend the
darkness that resides, for that
light which allows me to see. I
empower myself to experience
love innately present within.
I release my suffering, the
disconnection from love, so
my true life can begin. I am
willing to walk the path of a
few to experience that love.
So, I must drop the addiction
to fear to satisfy what I
long. I will remind others,
whoever they may be, there
is a love beyond eternity
that will set the spirit free.

In the Void

In the void of my mind, there is a connection. In the void, I am aligned with the source. In these moments, I am one with all things. In these moments, I hear from my soul, there are no questions of life. In these moments, fears are no more. No cares of past lives or perspectives of me; in these moments, I am whole. Regardless of life experiences and despite what I once believed, to see the truth of the Creator's love is to see what the Creator sees. It does not see a lowly peasant or a soul that is unclean, but a living extension of itself manifesting realities.

No Ills

Universal wisdoms open my
mind. I am free to examine
life from a higher side. The
moons and stars appear to
me, saying this is the way
of your reality; you are the
divine, and this is your truth;
the light within us is the
same within you. Child of
humanity, revive your name
and create in the world a
light without shame. Look
within and speak your truth.
Stardust and sunlight flow
through you. The universe
bears no ill toward you. All
are one and love is absolute.

A Seer's Prayer

Angels connect me to the
field of love and awaken its
wisdom within me; open my
awareness to the power it has,
so its light can shine through
me. Boldly empower my
sight to see what others may
not see; awaken my heart to
the power of love inherently
present in me. Broaden my
path in a way that is pure
in an essence that is divine,
and bring me to that special
place where my spirit freely
shines. Touch my feet with a
joyful dance that reflects the
rhythm of the stars. May it
guide my feet with an energy
that rises above all harm.
Align me with a frequency
the source alone can use.
Let love be the melody of
my heart's natural tune.

I Am Her Child

She taught me the stories
of my lifetimes in the cave
of creation. There I learned
what stood before me and
what I am here to do. Though
I walked the earth but a few
times, she remembers me.
She holds all my memories.
She calls me by my name the
divine speaks in light, and
remembers all of my footsteps
and incarnations of every
life. A conduit of breath she
is to me; and a mother, she
will always be. I may be a
child of the stars, but when
I am here, I am Gaia's child.

Universal Source

You created the universe
with your will and intent;
by your power, the moons
manifest. By endowing your
light and the presence of
love, consciousness became
known to all. The stars in the
skies and the herds below
are all extensions of thee.
The sun, the air, the land,
and the seas, in harmony
with you, they sing. I honor
you as I honor myself, as I
find your reflection in me.
So, I extend my presence as
an extension of love until
I am home with thee.

Lady of the Moon

Your presence touches my
spirit as I see you in the
skies. At times, I think of
you. Joyful tears I have cried,
celestial radiant spirit with
a light that lifts mankind,
reaching out to all who will
accept and not deny. Dear
goddess of light, I feel you in
my soul, bringing healing
energies that make my spirit
soar. You have shown me new
perspectives, new realities,
and the significance of a
world that is merely a dream.
You showed me stories that
my eyes could not perceive.
I know you as a healer, a
revealer of many things.

A World in Me

Through my spirit, I create harmony with the energy of creation. Creativity flows through me. My manifestations reflect the pull of the moon as new realities gravitate to me. I am the sun, in an endless expression vibrating through eternity. The universe is one with me, expressed by a world within me. I am balance. I am peace. I am love. I am light.

Cosmic Truths

Who do I tell the things that I know?
The experience I have should I let
it go? Who would understand?
Where do I begin? I am the I Am.
How does that sink in? Dear Beings
of Light, the records you keep carry
the essence of the source. Why did
you let me see? They awakened my
memories and aligned my soul to
see the cosmic destinies physical
eyes cannot perceive. Dear Keepers
of the Knowing, what did I become?
The energy I find feels like the light
of one thousand suns. Can I hold
this frequency in my biology? Its
data carries eternities that flow
like living seas. My higher self now
speaks. A master lives in me. As I
spoke, I heard his voice. Oh, how
could this be? I have unknowingly
lived a lie. Filters burden me. The
beliefs I thought were me hid my true
identity. You have broken the mold
of my passivity as I stand in the light
of truth you have revealed to me. Oh,
what man am I? How could I not see?
All of this time, divinity lives in me.

CHAPTER 2

THE WORLD BEHIND THE VEIL

Love Dances

She dances in the stars way up in the skies.
She hopes to awaken love. She hopes to
spread its light. She is sensitive to the pains
that plague humanity. So, she dances to
spark a light, hoping one might become free.
Her moves spread an energy that speaks
to the heart. It says love is all around, but
inside is where it starts. Connect with
the presence of love that resides within. It
fills every void and brings your suffering
to an end. Accept the love within, and
your heart becomes alive, spreading light
in your darkness, where you find you are
divine. She dances through the cosmos.
Her messages shine bright. She encourages
every soul to look inside and find the light.

The Priestess Sings

She sings the answers, and
she sings with grace. She
sings to empower the whole
human race. Like an arcangel,
her foundation is love. She
has the heart of a prophet
and the peace of a dove. She
sings a melody that shines the
light. It awakens the world
with divine insights. Her
melodies shift nations as she
sings her tunes. Her rhythm
opens hearts to embrace new
truths. She sings a song that
heals the pain. She enlightens
minds, breaking shackles
and chains. She frees the
heart in wonderful ways.
As she sings and dances,
freedom is proclaimed.

Night Skies Shine Truth

Celestial bodies in the sky, telling stories way up high. Conscious lights in the depths of space speak unto the human race, igniting all with perspectives and truths. There is a new earth with a brighter tune, where all aligns with a common good: a place where pure souls are most understood. A consciousness from a higher place creates a most harmonious state: a place where inventions revolutionize the day, and creativity expands at a faster rate. There is a new earth that is here for you, aligned with the stars for a collective good. Love is the light the stars shine on you in a bond connected beyond distance or moods. Starry night skies hold many truths, a divine reflection of the universe and you.

The Piper Plays

The piper plays his tune, and
his sound ignites creation.
His tune creates new worlds,
and it changes the tone of
nations. The beauty of his art
is collective transformation,
as his rhythms have uprooted
the greatest of civilizations.
He plays throughout the
cosmos, and some call him
by his name. He has forever
played his tune, a constant
melody known as change.

Gaia Dances

As the sun rises, she
dances. New energies have
appeared. It is light covering
the earth. Vision is getting
clear. Many are beginning
to see. Awareness comes
more naturally. She knows
the days are closer when
the earth is truly free. As
the moons bring changes
and restart new energies,
a new sun rises, bringing
darkness to its knees. With
a cheerful heart, she dances,
and it shifts realities while
the stars sing prophecies
of when the world is free.

A Bond with Nature

There was a time when things
on Earth were connected beyond
limitation. Humans, elves, and
fairies were merely aspects of nature.
The animals held their place and
were regarded as sentient beings.
The oceans, air, and land spoke
to all the conscious creatures.
All understood their place and
connection to one another in a
system that made them extensions of
each other. Interdimensional beings
supported this sacred state, deeply
connected to Gaia in a bond to keep
Earth safe. This arrangement was
unbreakable in every single feature.
Even if forgotten the bond still
thrives within all creatures. When
one decides to change their pace,
slow down, and connect with nature,
an innate connection is felt within
their biological makeup. There is
magic awaiting every single seeker,
as in the essence of Mother Nature,
one finds their greatest teacher.

CHAPTER 3

THE FEMININE DIVINE

Our Mother Prayer

Our Mother, who dwells in all things: honor and reverence to you. Thy way is life. Thy guidance is light and blessing. For the land and the seas and the air we breathe, we thank you. Lead us not into separation, but guide us into unity. For thy will is harmony, balance, love, oneness, and togetherness. Amen.

As She Speaks

She feels the world changing
as she uses her voice.
Atmospheres begin to shift.
She aligns with her source.
Her vibrations flow with a
beautiful power that goes
beyond herself. Many are
inspired. Her words are like
fire that melts the hardest
chains, like sunlight in the
skies that dries up all the
rain. She finds passion and
strength in the use of her
words. She speaks new truths
that have yet to be heard.
Liberation runs rampant
as her truths are revealed.
In the presence of her light,
many are healed. Forever
blessed is the Feminine
Divine who has come to
find that God lives inside.

Nature Soul

Her spirit dances in nature.
The earth calls out her
name. The plants tell her
their secrets. Gaia's magic
runs through her veins. She
is a divine soul. Her light
creates change. She came
to remind us all. Mother
Earth can heal our pains. She
spends her time in the forest,
grounded with the earth.
Angelic energy surrounds
her. The ancestors praise her
work. She has the light of a
healer. Her teachings help
us see that nature has the
remedy to heal humanity.

Moon Goddess

The depths of the ocean and
the freedom of the tides are
inside her. She aligns herself
with the moon. Her body
houses the light, as it is home
for her divine consciousness.
Though her body is but a
vessel, her light shines. In
the darkest of places, she
shines. For those who have
lost their way, she shines.
For her truth, is the light
and divinity is in her ways.

Her Eyes

The beauty of her eyes is
that she sees many things.
Divinity is in her blood. The
Earth Realm is her dream.
Born of air and fire, with
depths like the seas, she sees
the beauty of the land. She
sees herself in all things.
Her hands exude healing.
Her light is like the stars, a
creator at heart. She is an
expression of love. Blessings
are in her presence. Her
words create heaven. She is
the goddess of dreams. She
sees a world that is unseen.

Sacred Image

When she found her inner source, she found her sacred image. Her heart expanded wide. It was a time of new beginnings. She found her sacred image in the light that she saw herself. It liberated her soul beyond what words could express. Her crown shined like stars. Peace became her necklace. Abundance became her covering. Self-love became her headdress. She embodied who she was. Her truth was in her image. She embraced a new life through an unprecedented new beginning.

Her Eyes Revealed Her Soul

She saw the changes in the
world. She saw the flaws. The
flaws were the things that
were disconnected from love.
The mere sight of these flaws
made her observant and
quiet. She was an empath,
and many did not understand
her ways. They just knew
that she was different. Her
eyes told her story. They said
things that her mouth did
not communicate. What
her eyes saw, the world
could not understand. She
was a love child. She was
blessed by the moon, and
it was her gift to love.

A Star in the Night

She was a beautiful soul,
transitioning through
realities in her life. She was
envied by those around her.
There were many who sought
to dismiss her light, but
she could not be dismissed.
Her purpose was divinely
ordered to be; and when
they rose against her, she
awakened to new wisdoms
and to new understandings
that empowered her light.
She awakened to new
insights that caused her
to transcend, for she could
never be diminished. She
was the star in the night,
creating new worlds in
the midst of the darkness.
When they tried to pursue
her, they found themselves
guided by her light.

A Challenge to Receive

She sat in the garden in a
moment of self-reflection,
seeking to uncover the root
of her dissatisfaction. Her
wants and desires had evaded
her; no matter how hard she
tried. Her heart ached for
answers as she wondered the
reason why. She soon came
upon a flower. It reminded
her of herself. The flower was
stunning and vibrant. It was
growing wild and needed no
help. She suddenly began to
weep. She felt clarity inside,
as her had heart unraveled
an unsuspected surprise.
With no pursuit for sunlight,
and no effort to create the
rain, the flower had all it
needed. The flower suffered
no pain. She saw herself
through the flower. In this
reflection, she could see. In
the purity of stillness, one
receives what they need.

A Higher Side

A relationship that never
dies and guidance that never
rests. That is the connection
she has. It is with her higher
self. Some call it intuition
or a spark of the Most High.
To her, it is a friend and a
bridge to the other side.
She sees her own reflection
in the wisdom it provides.
She is connected to all
things through this voice
that lives inside. It provides
continuous guidance, and
its direction is never wrong.
She learned to trust it
more, and the connection
became more strong. She
found there is no end to its
abilities, and restrictions
are not required. It can
guide through anything. She
learned to trust her friend,
the one that lives inside. It
is called her higher self, and
its connection never dies.

Her Awakening

As she awakened, she came
to hear the voice of Spirit.
She began to notice a
conscious presence of life in
all things. The rivers, lakes,
and streams spoke to her,
and as she walked, she could
feel an awareness in the
land around her. She began
to communicate with the
elements and she obtained
wisdoms that inspired her.
She felt loved and supported
during these times. At some
point, it all appeared to be
a path guiding her into the
knowledge of self, as she
was made aware of the true
essence of who she was.
She was a fragment of the
creative source, discovering
herself in all things.

The Woman and the Tree

On the cool side of the tree,
there is love and there is
light. On the cool side of the
tree, she finds balance with
the sun's light. A different
kind of peace is what the
tree provides. She sees a
spiritual nature beyond
the tree's physical side. The
tree gives her clarity, and
her troublesome thoughts
subside, providing space for
her intuition to innately rise.
There is a well of abundance
and purity inside. In every
atom of the tree, a conscious
awareness ignites. On the
cool side of the tree, she finds
harmony with the light. On
the cool side of the tree, she
finds connection and insight.

The Night Revealed Her Soul

She found her memories
at the ocean, where the
water meets the moon. In
the darkness of night, she
discovered her soul. Away
from the crowd, and away
from the noise: that was the
place where her spirit was
made whole. In the night of
her own journey, far away
from home is where she found
love. That is where she found
her source. On a calm quiet
night, where the water meets
the moon, she found her own
light and the love for her soul.

A Rising Light

She was afraid of herself and, in many ways, she was un-accepting of her power. She was taught that her gifts of mediumship and clairvoyance were not good. Deep inside, she rejected herself. Perhaps this was the influence behind her thoughts of unworthiness or her inability to attract true love. For many moons, she was at war with herself on a subliminal level. All the while thinking her self-suppression was the right way to be. However, a time of change would come. Self-imprisonment was not aligned with her destiny, and false illusions of unworthiness could not stay. As the sun rises to shine its light, so does her spirit. Like the essence of a rebirth, her spirit arose to shine an inner clarity that dissolved her illusions and aligned her back home to love. In the acceptance of her differentness, the manifestation of her true power was born.

Ascension Is Her Dance

She dances with a freedom
that liberates her soul. She
ascends above all narratives
with a truth to behold. The
essence of her aura shines
like the queens of old. She
is the wisdom of a priestess
whose story is untold. She
dances in ascension with a
light that reveals. The sight
of her glory, false narratives
could not steal. She was
written out of scriptures that
denied her rightful place, as
patriarchal views discredit
the power in her ways. She is
the original keeper of wisdom
that guided humanity. The
Earth begins to rise as her
light sets all free. Goodbye,
old world. Her truth is made
known. Goodbye, old world.
Her face reflects the source.

Galactic Goddess

Her eyes tell stories. Her aura
sings, "Divine." Her vibe is
beyond this world. It awakens
hearts and minds. Brilliant is
her light. She awakens souls
to see, just being herself, a
sentient star-being. Galactic
is her nature. The stars are
her seas. She travels through
space and time to manifest
into being. The divine galactic
soul came to make a change.
The presence of her light
ensures that things are
not the same. The galactic
goddess shines. There are
worlds in her light. She is the
breath of galaxies and the
star that lights the night.

The Path of Her Difficulties

She walked the path alone. She had to, as she did not have a choice. So, she walked. She was carrying the loss of much, but she walked. Guided by her own light, she had to strengthen her own heart. Over time she felt herself change, but she had no reason to stop. So, she walked. She eventually came to a river many could not cross. She was unknowing of who she was, but she stood tall. As she walked over to the river, the waters began to part. She walked nearly to the end, but then she stopped. She wondered why the waters would part, knowing so many had to stop. "What was the difference?" she thought, as this one question pulled at her heart. She then looked up at the waters only to see there was a majestic phoenix; a sight she could not believe. It was a mystical creature she had never before seen. She then walked closer to the waters and realized the Phoenix was she.

Starseed Priestess

The cosmos sings her story.
Her awareness expands wide.
Limitations do not confine
her. She carries a sound mind.
She manifests with precision.
She captivates her dreams.
Much power rests inside her.
She knows she is a queen.
She embodied self-love when
she came to know herself.
It awakened the gifts inside
her. Insecurities were put to
rest. Now she tells her story
as the master of her soul.
The truth that lives inside
her makes her spirit bold.
Today she firmly stands,
with a light to behold. She
fulfills a path of destiny with
a fire that fuels her soul.

Mary Magdalene

An enlightened teacher taught with grace. A soul who inspired the human race, sharing an abundance of truths to awaken the world beyond reproof. Sacred knowledge ignites her heart. She carries the wisdom of the stars, but diminished to a harlot to ensure the world forgets her truths. A divine high priestess brought the light, teaching physical connection through spiritual enlightenment, as intimacy is a sacred gift for all to experience healing and bliss. Her wisdom empowered the greatest of men to become living sacraments and align with the divine inside, transcending fear for a divine mind. A higher nature is our truth. Masters awakened because of you, and so I write this poem for you. The divine high priestess whose light brought truth.

The Rising Priestess

The priestess awakens. It is her time to reign. The dawn of a new rising brings forth brighter days. The world has seen dark times, and truth now appears. Once buried by the darkness, now the light makes it clear. The water bearer comes to ensure a golden age. He swiftly removes the veil, putting all on the same page. There was an age of darkness and the world was ruled by fear. He brings an age of light, as ascension is here. The priestess awakens in the essence of a dove. She ushers in a world where the agenda is love.

CHAPTER 4

THE MASCULINE DIVINE

Masculine Divine

He walks in his integrity.
He walks throughout the
land, meditating with the
Earth, uplifting those that
he can. He is awakened in
his spirit, and he finds his
Promised Land. He dedicates
himself to the community
he has. Wise in his ways,
yet loves with his heart.
He ignites a soul with his
kind remarks. Arise, divine
man, to live above the mark.
Your light vibrates high; it
makes change come about.

He Shines

A man who sees God finds
the truth within himself. He
understands the role of love
and nothing else compares.
His love expands like
mountains, adding beauty to
the land. Majestic is the sight.
To witness is truly grand. He
deeply cares for others and
enlightens humanity. He
freely shines his light. It tells
his destiny. Renewed by the
waters, his wisdom is vast
as seas. Healing reflects his
nature. He shines divinity.

The Master

As he advanced in his
journey, many things became
clear. He began to see his
insecurities and weaknesses
as opportunities to grow. He
challenged them head-on to
the point that he obtained
mastery of them. He saw
every challenge as a stepping
stone leading him to a greater
awareness of himself. He saw
his path of life as a journey of
self-discovery, one that was
leading him to his highest
state of consciousness: a state
of greater manifestations,
and a place where he would
ultimately build his legacy.
It was his journey of life, one
that he was bound to master.

The Spiritual Man

A soul that is divinely
connected, he sees life
through a different lens.
Deeply connected with
spirit, his devotion has no
end. He broke the chains of
ego, for his heart could not
rest. He challenged all the
odds and found God within
himself. He exchanged his
suffering with love. He now
honors his higher self. He
masters the energy inside,
acknowledging spirit in every
breath. The Divine Masculine
shines. Though the world
experiences change, his
wisdom creates balance, and
his love breaks all chains.

A Soul Reborn

An old soul was reborn. He
was a master from the past
living in a modern world. He
felt a longing in his heart,
or so he thought. What he
really desired was to express
the magic that was hidden
in his soul. In a world that
had lost knowledge of how
men should be, the old soul
was a misfit. He was the
embodiment of a magic long
forgotten. Nonetheless, his
soul had returned. He came
to awaken the world to truth,
a truth that would awaken
souls, a truth that would
ignite the will to be free. The
old soul carried a gift, and
the truth of his gift was love.

Divine Man Divine Purpose

He walks in his power,
unpersuaded by society.
He is mindful of the snares
that undermine his divinity.
Conscious of his path and
mindful of his time, he
communes with the world
of spirit and awakens hearts
and minds. He exudes the
light of love and lives within
his truth. He is divinely
guided. Spirit shows him
what to do. He transcends a
carnal mind and defines his
moral code; he is free within
himself. His life attracts his
joys. Intuition stands beside
him. He has no need for force.
He is aware of his power. He
is aligned with his source.

When a Man Finds God

He rises above identity
and the ego faces death.
In the light of his greatest
awareness, he sees his higher
self. He finds his greatest
truths. All fears set sail.
He knows his true power,
and for that, he cannot fail.
Waters activate his anointing.
Sacred oil removes all veils.
He finds the essence of God
living within himself. His
presence enlightens others.
A great joy is felt. He holds
his own power, seeing the
truth for himself. His wisdom
honors love as divinity at its
best; as love is a power he
compares to nothing else.
Through love he serves, and
through love he heals. His
words move mountains and
make miracles appear.

CHAPTER 5
SOUL FLAMES

Soul Union

He is a shelter of love. He
keeps her heart in an open
place. She is a shining light.
She is the smile that lights
his face. Her wisdom and
her grace allow him to see.
His vision is expanded, he
learns who he can be. He
is a pillar of peace. She is
empowered by his touch. She
is the jewel in his crown. Her
value gifts him much. He
never stands alone. Her love
stands with him. She is the
earth. He is the ground. There
is harmony within them.

Soul Relations

She walks in her highest
power. She is nurtured by
his love. She has all she
can desire. She is secure in
her self-love. His wisdom
provides her fortress. His
balance unveils her grace.
Their spiritual connection
solidifies intimate bonds
they make. He is empowered
by her love. He masters his
inner world. The light that
he provides her is more
valuable than pearls. They
create new dimensions and
profound realities. In each
other, they find reflections
of their own divinity.

The Beauty of a Moment

In the sunlight, they sat,
admiring the greenery that
was around them. Sitting
on the grass, watching the
movement of the streams
flow by, he held her close
and lightly began to speak
affirmations of peace. The
sound of his voice soothed
her soul. The subtle sincerity
in conjunction with the
stability of his balanced
energy satisfied her desire
for harmonious company.
These conditions allowed her
spirit to shine freely, from
an organic place, without
restraint. She received his
affirmations deeply, and
without a kiss or a touch,
intimacy was attained.

His Thoughts

He was tired of the
societal flow of life and
the monotonous cycles of
romantic love. He wanted
more. There were many
beautiful women, but they
were disconnected from
their souls. His heart longed
for something different. He
smiled at the thought of a
woman who had an altar, one
who was in tune with nature.
Many nights he imagined
holding her under the stars
while reading each other's
past lives. Thoughts like this
kept him going. Inside, he
secretly vowed to honor the
days when he found her.

Divine Flames

There were times when we
were two humans. There were
times we were two oak trees,
rising high in the sun without
a concept of a need. There was
a time when we had no form,
and we watched the world
begin. Another time, we were
two earth masters balancing
the elements from within.
In every moment I found
you, I knew it was destiny.
Many paths our souls have
chosen; there was never an
uncertainty. I am inspired by
the memories that connect
us consciously. They carry
so much love; they unite us
spiritually. I embrace the
essence of divine ecstasy.
You could never be forgott ---
as you live inside of me.

Musings of a Divine Masculine

Unlike many others, he
sought after her innermost
being. He yearned to nurture
the parts of her that lived
behind the walls, the filters,
and the image. He desired the
parts of her that remained
unknown, even to her. The
parts she hid from others
were also hidden from
herself. His insight showed
him much, and his desires
were to nurture her softness.
Inside, he felt it was the
uncharted beauty of her
spirit. In her vulnerability, his
strength was made known.
The beauty he desired was
not in her body, but the
intrinsic truth of her soul.

She Lifts Him Up

His mind is on his mission and the vision he must manifest. He does not stand alone. He has divine help. As every kingdom has a queen that brings out the King's best, every man has an empire that deserves nothing less. As he walks his soul's journey, frustrations come to test. Her voice rings inside, reminding him of his best. She speaks to his soul, saying, "King, pursue your quest. The vision you have inside is greater than yourself. Stand tall, dear King. The Divine stands with thee. No power in this world can stop your destiny." She anoints his head with honor and speaks to his innermost place. He is fortified in his calling. His divinity is embraced. He sees the Creator in her and its reflection in himself. His empire materializes as she speaks to his higher self. She knows the man he is, and the encouragement she gives awakens his inner calling and ensures that his vision lives.

Divine Realities

She dances in his heart
space. His soul belongs to
her. She desires no one else.
His energy comforts her. He
embodies her desires. They
connect vibrationally. She
is a reflection of his spirit.
There is no place else he
would rather be. The highest
vibration of love exists on
a spiritual plane. It carries
many secrets. Much power
is obtained. When souls
are unified, they expand in
harmony. Life unveils the
secrets of divine realities.

Uniting Flames

She is the water. He is the
land. Their presence creates
life. The source expands itself
as the two of them unite.
Wisdom meets power when
the two of them combine. A
new world is born, leaving the
ordinary behind. She expands
in her full glory. Her higher-
self shines. His inner gifts
are unleashed. His chakras
fully align. They release their
inhibitions. They become the
essence of one, uniting as one
flame that cannot be undone.
A conjunction in the cosmos
aligns with greater times.
They experience the heaven
of two souls that unite.

Love Aligns

Her fearlessness of love
matched the fearlessness of
his heart; and when they were
together, their whole world
seemed to change. She could
not have a bad day while he
was around. Similarly, he
felt the smoothness of their
connection put his mind in
a state of ease. They were
rejuvenated by each other.
This perspective made
them both smile. The high
of the vibes and the flow of
their natural energy was
something they could not
give up. To them, this was
priceless. Their combined
presence was their heaven.
A world their hearts alone
could define. A place more
priceless than space and time.

A Sacred Exchange

As he held her, he considered her needs. He was carrying every intent to heal her soul. Although she was not consciously aware of his intentions, she could feel the vibe was different. The energy felt most comfortable, like home. Every breath brought them closer. Though it was more than soothing physical needs. What they created at that moment took them beyond an eternity. Void of meaningless motion, every movement began to heal. Past traumas were being removed. Past pains were being healed. All in a single moment, she felt her heart began to lift. He created a magical moment, simply by his intent. He put aside his thoughts, and he cleared his mind. At that moment, he was a vessel for his inner divine. His intuition led his touch. He saw what he needed to do. At the moment, she could not talk; the energy felt new. He was guided by love. He showered her desires like rain. The act created sacred vibrations that took away their pains. The act of healing her created healing for himself. Her divine feminine energy put his soul at rest. He released his pains. Some had yet to be revealed. He was uncertain of what had happened, yet he knew something was healed. There was no sense of time. They felt their spirits leave. They wondered how it could be real. They did not know that love could heal.

CHAPTER 6

THE DIVINITY WITHIN

The Silence Inside

Silence the mind and connect
with the one who lives inside.
There reside all answers one
could ever find. An inherent
divine nature is the truth
that you will find, amid the
silence, the silence inside.

The Profundity of a Soul

Your very steps are ordered
and aligned with destiny.
Every move you make is
captured in Gaia's memory.
You are known by a name that
is spoken in light; a name the
divine calls out from a world
beyond human sight. Though
separated by the veil between
spirit and mankind, you are
a shining light that expands
beyond space and time. Your
condition is profound. Though
you may not see your truth,
the vibration of creation
exists in harmony with you.

Miracles and Truth

With every given miracle, you
can find a hidden truth. At
any moment, one can happen
as the power resides in you.
To create new worlds and
manifest realities was a gift
of the masters who found
their divinity. Embrace your
path to truth. You will find
it all within. The courage to
shine your light guarantees
that you will win. Know
that you are able, and you
deserve the very best. Things
begin to happen when you
believe in yourself. You
have the power to create
and to make your dreams
come true. The miracles
you seek live inside of you.

Beautiful You

Your strength is beautiful,
and your confidence is pretty.
You embody self-love, and the
sight empowers many. Your
light is bright. You are a gift
to behold. The energy you
carry is food for the soul. You
know that you are special,
and you found your self-
worth. You are the essence
of breakthroughs and divine
rebirths. The strength that
you have propels you higher. It
is the fuel that also manifests
your desires. Love who you
are and who you have become.
Your light is magnificent, and
your time has just begun.

Embrace Your Truth

Now is the time for all to search their hearts and connect with the truth inside. That is where it all starts. We carry the inner power to manifest a greater world. Know that you are more than any words you have ever heard. Fearlessly love yourself, and magic you will find. You can create your own world. The universe does not deny. Please release your doubts. They only hold you back. Know that you are capable. There is nothing that you lack. You are an extension of divinity, and that is your living truth. The power of heaven and earth manifest themselves through you.

You Just Might Be

The man desired change. By his faith, he counted it done, but what he did not know was how the change would come. The change came with challenges. He knew this could be the case, but he did not know it would cost all of his favorite things. It would take his favorite car. It would take his favorite friends. It would take his favorite beliefs, the ones held deep within. He was disgruntled by his challenges, though he knew he needed change. He could not have his victories if he chose to remain the same. So, he decided to let them go, all of his favorite things; and shortly after he did, the whole world began to change. He saw himself as just a man, and there was something he could not see: he was carrying a destiny that would set the masses free. What he saw as personal challenges brought the world a victory. As a master of the elements lived within this being. So never doubt yourself because you just might be the undiscovered catalyst to set this whole world free.

Subconscious Awareness

She sat on the edge of the bed, listening to music and enjoying her thoughts in solitude. She began to drift off; and before she knew it, she was fast asleep. She found herself in a world where there were several versions of herself simultaneously existing all at once. It was as if the fabric of time bent, allowing her to see all her past lives and future incarnations. As she watched, she felt emotions rushing through her awareness. An essence of wisdom seemed to flow through her many lives and experiences. There were no words to reflect the infinity of what she was. Suddenly, she woke up. She was left knowing that she was truly limitless, and the experience she called life was a singular expression of a continuous experience that her higher awareness created.

Self-Love

Happiness aligns with those who come to
love themselves. They rise like the eagle
that soars through the air. The divine
empowers them through a love that shines
within. By obtaining self-love, many battles
are effortless wins. They discover their
foundation. A truth that lives within, having
found the secret where true love begins.
Many have decided they do not need to look
within. Why work to find self-love when you
can just pretend? So, they neglect self-love,
and they neglect to heal, thinking, "What
could be the difference? It is really no big
deal." So, they miss the magic and bear un-
needed stress. They did not find self-love and
did not come to know themselves. They have
not found the foundation that empowers
one within. So, they battle the outside
world, unknowing their battles are within.

Lover's Light

There is a fire that burns
within, its light is to behold.
It is the lover's light, shining
bright, connecting kindred
souls. Its warmth radiates
through those who have the
capacity to love. It opens
the eyes with divine insight
giving wisdom from above.
The fire shares its secret with
those who learn its ways. It
opens doors to the knowing
of a magic that does not fade.
There is a fire that burns
within. It lives inside the soul.
Those who find its secrets,
learn a joy that is untold.

Weirdiful

Some may think you are
weird, which means you are
very special. You defy the
mundane with your natural
essence. You are unique,
like a diamond. That makes
you hard to find. They sum
you up as weird because you
cannot be defined. You are
custom-made and uniquely
one of a kind. Your difference
makes you beautiful. You
are a pearl in a sea of time.
Shooting stars ignite the
skies when all others stay in
place. You are not the usual
kind, and that is the magic
that makes you great.

Find Your Divine

Your worth is a value held
deep inside, and at times
you may not see it. You may
intimidate others and not
know why. Beloved, they
can see you. Never devalue
your worth. It is your inner
truth. One may hide many
things, but do not hide the
magic of you. No matter how
different you are, embrace
whatever you find. The truth
of divinity is not outside.
It lives inside of you.

Freedom

Love is what you become in
the very absence of fear. It
awakens a soul's truth to find
a love so dear. It purifies the
heart. The moment one sees is
to know the meaning to love,
unconditionally. Love is the
vein that brings meaning to
life. Its power creates shifts
and brings profound insight.
To see the world through love
that flows organically is to
see life the way the Creator
wanted you to see. Free from
illusions. Free from a world of
fear. Free to be who you are
without resistance standing
near. To release the weight of
fear and obtain true clarity is
to witness the very moment
when a soul becomes free.

CHAPTER 7

CONSCIOUSNESS SHIFTS

A New Sun Rises

The walls are falling down.
They separated who was
who. Intermingling the dark
and the light, could not tell
a lie from the truth. A new
sun rises, shining light on
the inner truth, revealing
those who do not have love in
mind, and the difference from
those who do. Shine, light,
shine! The world has been
waiting for you. Shine, light,
shine! Your origin is truth.

New Occasions

We are rising to new
occasions. Nothing can
stop the flow. Forget about
the past: it does not exist
anymore. New Events are
coming. Get ready to receive.
Release your fears and doubts
to obtain new victories. We
are building a new world.
It is awaiting you. Connect
with your inner truth: it
reflects the road for you.
When you walk your highest
path, intuition guides you
through. Abundance is a
friend that is there to support
you. A greater world emerges.
It brings new destinies. It
awakens those who sleep to
a world where all are free.

When the Sun Sat High

When the sun sat at the top of the sky, the world received amazing surprises. Many thought they knew the false from the real, and this was the case until the truth was revealed. It showed perspectives they did not know, and they realized they fell for a singular show, created by a few who chose to deceive, as false perceptions gave them much to achieve. The illusions and constructs were far removed, and the people came to find their own truths. All were divided and to all unknown, but the divided and conquered became united and strong. Wealth began to flow. The youth came to prosper. They abolished old systems and were no longer slaughtered. For all had suffered, and all were deceived. When the sun sat high, it was easy to see. So, they ended their sufferings and healed their disease: a radical change, even the gods esteemed.

New Energy Calls

A new day has come for those
that see. It is time to reflect
on your energy. The higher
you vibrate, the more you
create. New energies are here
to usher in a new day. So,
arise to your calling: you have
waited for your part. It is time
to stand true to what lies in
your heart. There is more to
come; do not be deceived. It
is time to mind the things
you believe. If living through
your passions manifests your
dreams, now is the time to do
whatever you need. Holder
of light, seeker of truth,
these days are your days.
These moments are for you.

Rebirth

Liberate all souls beyond the
illusions of differences. Unite
us all as one. Enlighten our
consciousness. Bring us to
the place that connects us to
love. Manifest it in our hearts;
create harmony with all.
Honor the truth that unites
humanity; no matter who you
are, you extend from divinity.
Bring us to the place where
all can be free in spirit and
in heart and a new reality.
A place without judgment, a
place where all can see that
every soul they meet is but
a reflection of thee. Unite
us all as one, in our highest
destinies. A great evolution
indeed, a rebirth of humanity

A Change in Times

In comes the shift, creating one side and
another. You have the paradigms of an old
world and the new energy of another. There
is a perspective you can find. It challenges
the mind, as it subconsciously equates to
people choosing sides. The paradigms of
an old world and new energy of another.
Divinity on one side, fear on the other. It
is seeing God beyond the systems created
by men versus finding God for yourself
through a path you walk within. It is
finding the divinity innately kept inside
or following old traditions and paradigms
that coincide. The world begins to change
as the age of light arises. It removes the
illusions and annihilates the lies. What
path will one take? Patriarchal paradigms,
or will one seek to find the divinity inside?

You Decide

When the time has come for
an old world to end, what
will you be doing, my friend,
avoiding transitions to make
the world better or doing your
part to create a new heaven?
Whatever you decide, let it be
for the better. The climate is
changing, and it is not about
the weather. You must decide
just where you will be: rising
in love or reaping bad seeds.
Oh, the unwanted harvests
you personally created, all
because love was negated.
The world is changing. What
will you do, go out with the
old or bring in the new? The
time has come; here stands
a new day. Will you give love
a try or deny with old ways?

CHAPTER 8

BEARERS OF THE LIGHT

A New World Rises

Awaken, children, awaken!
The time has come for you
to shine. You have toiled for
so long waiting for peace of
mind. The magic happens
when you create. It has
always been inside you.
When you awaken from your
slumber, that is when the
magic finds you. Awaken,
children, awaken! Your world
is yours to claim. Awaken,
children, awaken! It will
never be the same again.

The Lives of a Healer

Heal the wounds that lay
inside. It is time to awaken
from your past lifetimes. They
hurt you, disowned you, and
kept you outside. They said
you were too different. They
said, "Go and hide." A blessing
you were, though they could
not see. Many great things
laid hidden in thee until
you were needed, then they
could see. At those times you
were worshiped, because
you healed their disease.
Awaken old soul. It is okay
to be you. You must shine
your light, and you must
speak your truth. Awaken,
old soul. They won't harm
you this time. The moment
has come. Arise and shine.

Children of Light

When the universe expands,
so do the hearts and minds
of men; they expand beyond
all barriers created. The
light of truth comes and
forces all to greatness, as love
can no longer be negated.
A generation has come to
end all cycles, supporting
the earth at all costs. Their
vibrations are highest. They
shine like the stars and are
known as the children of God.
They embody peace, while
others live in fear, believing
many illusions that appear.
The children of the light
work through the night to
deliver the planet from fear.

Lightworker

Some may get confused, saying
"It's not all love and light," though
your higher awareness speaks
from a place of greater insight.
The world is filled with contracts
many have come to fulfill. You
opted to come to earth and assist
on your free will. You carry a
natural countenance. Many do
not understand. Some may try to
mimic you, but longevity is not
in their plan. Because you are
the light, you came to empower.
Human consciousness is rising,
and your frequency brings much
power. You are your best version
simply being yourself. While
others proclaim their gifts, to
simply stand is your test. You walk
the path of a few, knowing what
you came to do; and with every
ridicule, the Divine advances you.
Arise, child of light. Your presence
creates change. There comes a new
earth, in which the light reigns.

Worlds We Create

We must create our art. We
must create our messages.
It separates us from
illusions, agendas, and false
testaments. Living through
our gifts satisfies our needs
and provides the world a light
that helps them see. Divine
is your nature. Know that
you were made complete. Tap
into what you have. You'll find
everything you need. One soul
can change the world. This
potential shines true. Your
gifts reflect God, and there
is a world in need of you.

A Lightworker's Receipt

I am ready for all things the
universe places in my path.
I know that I am worth it.
The storm clouds will not
last. I am ready to receive the
highest good in store for me.
I have no fears of aligning
with my highest destiny.
When it comes, I will not run.
When it appears, I will not
hide. I receive with gratitude.
I accept what is mine.

You Will Know the Way

No fear lightworkers, the
divine will show you the way.
You will find peace in the
storm by knowing the role
you play. You walk a higher
path with an expanded
point of view. You bring
new rays of light to a world
that needs your truth. A
new sun rises; discernment
holds the key. The bearers of
the light see a fine destiny.
No fear, lightworkers, your
intuition lights the way.
When intellectuals can
serve earth no more, your
light will lead the way.

Divinely Supported

Shifts will come into your
life. They can appear to be
everywhere. Do not neglect to
realize the magic that is there.
Changes may come, but it is
not to ruin your day. It is an act
of benevolence guiding you to
a greater place. Disregard the
thoughts that may come to rattle
the mind. Keep your mission
and goals in focus, and things
will be fine. Work through
the challenges or difficulties
you perceive. They carry great
purpose; they help manifest your
dreams. No worries of how you
look or what you have to show.
Just focus on your light and
the story will unfold. Trust and
believe abundance flows beyond
your needs. You are divinely
supported, and your success is
guaranteed. Spirit walks with
you in all that you go through.
Know that there are no limits, as
there are angels surrounding you.

Because You Made A Step

You made your transition.
You challenged the unknown.
You lost many friends, and
your relationship had to go.
You walked into the new to
align with your truth. You
went through all the pain for
the greater things you had to
do. You walked a challenging
road, not knowing where
to go; but as you made your
steps, spirit began to show.
Know that you arrived.
There is much in store, you
see. Walking the authentic
path was designed to set you
free. You will surely find, in
the moments you are still,
you are divinely guided and
your needs always fulfilled.
You walk a higher path. The
old one is done. You are the
alchemist that creates new
worlds, and your time has
just begun.

The Love Child

Dear love child, they do not know love like you. You came from an ascended planet to be a light that stands true. You carry a high vibration, and many will not understand. Neither do they know you hold destiny by the hand. Because you are a light, your path shows the way. In the theatre of life, you change the entire play. Fearlessly, shine your light. Inside you is the key. Your heart holds the frequency that uplifts humanity. Please stand tall. They cannot see like you. Do not expect all others to acknowledge what you do. Live by your truth. Your heart knows the way. Many are locked into the game when you come to make a change. Dear love child, they cannot see your truth. There is a brighter future that lives inside of you.

Starseed

You came to incarnate at a time of
need. You're embarking on a journey
that creates victories. Old souls carry
knowledge that surpass space and
time. You are aware of who you are,
and you do your job just fine. You
came to spread your light. You do it
with truths. You do it in your energy.
It is uniquely you. You came at a time
when you were needed most. You are
an angel in disguise. Your presence
brings them hope. You inspire many
with the things that you do. You
know who you are, and you choose
to live your truth. There is a shift, it
is true, and it happens due to you.
You are an extension of the divine
doing what you came to do. You are
awakening the masses. Ascension is
in your touch, and so you touch the
world. Your presence brings them
much. You awaken souls, wherever
you may be. You're the ascension that
was planted. It came as a Starseed.

Earth Angels Incarnate

The old soul, the shaman, it
is good to see you now. More
light is on the planet, and you
carry the torch around. Way-
shower, healer, this world
was made for thee. Intercede
on behalf of others, as they
benefit greatly, you see. Trust
your intuition as you grow
even more. The planet is
shifting tremendously. At this
point, the whole world knows.
Do your work, dear shaman.
Your work is needed, you see.
You are pulling the vibrations
that heal the planet's need.

When the Light Is Hardest to Find

There will be some obstacles
that appear within your path.
You must stay grounded;
the storm clouds will pass.
Trust that you are supported
when things go a difficult
way. Know that you are
surrounded; there will come
brighter days. If darkness
has its moment, illusions can
appear. In the stillness of a
moment, there is a peace that
is always there. Angels stand
in your shadow, they never
leave you behind. With every
challenging moment comes
the opportunity to shine.
Never doubt your ability,
dear extension of the Divine.
The highest vibrational
moments come when the
light is hardest to find.

No Fear Child of Light

The road may look uncertain;
trust no harm will come
your way. Know that you
are protected; put all fears
away. No harm comes near
thy dwelling; you carry a
special task. You are divinely
supported, so carry no fear
of lack. Angels stand by your
side and prepare the way for
thee. They are not dismayed
by obstacles as they prepare
your victories. Do not fear,
dear one, no harm to you
and yours. All is covered by
your blessings; the divine
has made it so. Focus on your
light. Know that your path
shines bright. An entourage
surrounds you and they
keep you in their sights.

Let It All Unfold

Do not anticipate the
journey; just enjoy the ride.
The inevitable will happen;
keep your eyes on the prize.
Your destiny supports you,
and those dreams will come
true. Trust the light inside
and always speak your
truths. Your mind, body, and
spirit hold divinity in place.
The power is inside you to
manifest your brighter days.
The physical world changes
when you speak your truths.
The Creator's love is inside
you, so heaven comes to
you. Do not worry about the
journey or how the story
goes. The material world will
bend. Just let it all unfold.

New Destinies

The path may seem arduous.
There are challenges at every
step. Evolution is the theme:
it will advance you through
the test. It is not designed to
be easy; it is designed to bring
out your best. When you align
with the truth inside, new
realities manifest. Release
your inhibitions and put all
fears aside. The power within
you is greater than anything
that resides outside. You have a
divine purpose. It is written in
the stars. You are magnificently
created to reflect the face of God.
Your nature carries no shame.
You are divinity at its best. The
source of all things sees you as
an extension of itself. Arise, dear
souls! Let your vibrations rise.
The frequency you have is a gift
from the Most High. Let your
light shine for all the world to
see. Ascension embraces your
hands. You shine new destinies.

Trust and Believe

There is no need to worry. All is as it should. You are not alone. Let this be understood. At times you may forget, and events may trouble you. Know that you are blessed. Things are working out as they should. Release all thoughts of pain, and fears of what may come. Trust that you are supported, and your better days have come. Awaken to the magic that is deep inside of you. You have gifts that fuel your dreams; they are waiting to come true. Know that you are special. There is more than you can see. Your miracles start to happen at the moment you believe.

CHAPTER 9

THE AGE OF AQUARIUS

The Age of Light

We are welcoming the
days when light is reborn.
It unifies the masses and
connects every soul. There
is a great awakening, at
a time that was foretold.
Humanity begins to rise into
the knowledge of its own. We
are overcoming systems and
breaking chains that bind.
We walk in a new awareness,
leaving fear and darkness
behind. A step into a new
world brings the experience
of light and truth, like the
divinity of the soul, for which
there is no substitute. An
awakening of the masses
enlightens everyone; all are
soon to realize that better
days have come. We are
moving into the knowledge
of our true divinity. A
world once blind enters the
times when all can see.

The Fall

When the light hits, the establishments will fall; for they are built upon foundations that were not based on love. As love becomes the way, all other things will fall, identified as nonsense, humanity will ignore. For all will see the light, shining in truth, as it identifies all snares and brings the wrongs' rebuke. As love becomes the way, it brings greater peace: no more mental constructs enslaving humanity. Love will break the chains; its light will let all see the divinity that resides within humanity. The greatest Masters spoke, saying, "God is within." The masses, duped by establishments say, "all are born of sin." Let every spell be broken, as an awakening takes place. You are extensions of the Creator and divinity is innate.

Light of Aquarius

Do not compare what is to
come to what has already
been. The light comes to take
you further. A new world
now begins. Open the doors
for change. A new earth
manifests; it brings with it
new energies comparable
with nothing else. Rise like
the sun. Greater things are
waiting for you. Open up your
heart to achieve a greater
view. Where we are set to
go, has not been seen before.
The stars have foretold a
brighter world unfolds.

Sudden Changes

Light uncovers what was
hidden in the dark. The tides
are beginning to turn, and
spirit knows every heart.
Many men have come and
deceived other men, but as
the light shines, darkness
comes to an end. The light
of truth has come, as it was
written in the stars a day
would come when the walls of
darkness would fall, freeing
all captives beyond what
many would believe. Every
dynasty came to end, which
none could have foreseen.
The time is upon us now,
as it was said to come. An
old world is ending now, in
the rising of a new sun.

New Realities

We are rising into a new reality. Things are falling into place. The light magnifies itself, expanding love in a whole new way. Our highest realities come when we release what does not serve; they bring us brighter days where our deepest truths are heard. In comes a new era, empowered by the heart. Many have come to assemble; they came to do their part. The light of love shines in places that have not seen, as it has never been the few. The masses create the collective dream. We enter a new awareness. The stars have fore told. Humanity comes to find the divine nature of the soul.

New World

The light moves in a fluid
motion, touching hearts
and minds, uniting itself
with some. Others choose
to be left behind. The light
continues to move, reaching
all who will receive. No one is
exempted; it came for all of
humanity. Those who receive,
move on to a better place,
finding inner peace and joy
that nothing can replace. To
accept is to change, and this
is how you start: embrace
a brand-new world by
accepting one in your heart.

Embrace Your Light

A new world emerges from beyond the view. It challenges every soul to find their own truths, as now we enter a time of change and things can no longer remain the same. As the light draws nigh, it brings many to wonder, as the world experiences new encounters. Some are in tune with the truth within, while others wonder when the madness will end. The light comes for those who are ready. So, keep your head high and keep your walk steady. Continuously forward is the new way, as continuous change is here to stay. The light within is your guide to truth. So, do not neglect the light within you. It serves as your guide in the midst of the rain, embrace or be lost in a magnitude of change.

Humanity Is at the Gates

Heaven opens its gates for
many to come through. Some
say it is love and light. Some
say it is witnessed by a few. As
the world begins to change
in the most significant ways,
many will embrace, and a few
remain the same. Invested
in old energy, not knowing
change would come, they will
run at every chance to stop a
rising sun. The universe has a
mandate, and a time was set
for change. Any effort to stop
that change only proliferates
the game. So, change comes,
and to all of humanity. It
does not skip a beat, and
every soul will see. For
these things must happen.
Radical change begins.
Humanity will not be down.
It is designed for all to win.

CHAPTER 10

PROPHECY & POETRY

The Grid-Worker Walks

He walks through the land
observing energies, quietly
shifting the grid to the
highest degree. He is aware
of the pains that plague
humanity. He opens new
portals so that balance
is achieved. A pouring of
energies aligns Earth with
the source. An advanced
acceleration throws old
energies off-course. In comes
a new world that could not
be foreseen, as unexpected
change shifts reality. He
calls the beings of light who
came to make a change. A
new sun rises and activates
their DNA. Gaia sets the
stage for the light to take its
place. Behold a new world
and a new human race.

Turn Goes the Table

Turn goes the table. Power shifts to different nations. What the world witnesses now is the falling of the matrix. They wave their media wand to find it is not favored, illusions have no power. A greater consciousness overtakes them. Turn goes the table. Was it all just a show? The true elect of God now appear and man their posts. Their designs were unstable. They disregarded divine nature, as order is restored through a great revelation. Turn goes the table. The elect have awakened. The walls of Babylon fall as they are torn from their foundation. A new sun rises. A new energy proceeds. It uplifts the world and no man can intervene. True power flows from a pure creative source. It creates new worlds by transforming the old. Turn goes the table. They are frantic and cannot take it. Balance is restored; and no man can make or break it.

Nature's Harmonious Tune

The wind of awakening runs
rampant like a breath of salvation,
freeing hearts and minds to
experience more. Deeper truths,
soul missions and divine inspiration
ignite like never before. The earth
rises in a new direction. Human
consciousness leaps to new heights.
Change takes place in a whole new
way as people worldwide unite.
New insights take hold, and new
realities unfold as the spirit of
humanity is reborn. Incomes a new
earth as the stars foretold. Balance
and enlightenment are restored.
Peace takes its place in organic
ways, as systems of destruction are
uprooted and replaced. Prosperity
and abundance, quench thirst
and hunger. Earth's true nature
is a beautiful state. Enlightened
minds shine. Their truths are
divine. New paradigms manifest
new times. Humanity finds the
truth that lives inside. Human
nature reflects the Divine.

Gaia's Angelic Seeds

To Gaia's angelic seeds, you do not know who you are. You were made for a singular purpose: to reflect the face of God. Seeded on the earth with a divine destiny, you are guardians of a planet that shares your biology. Many things have happened for you to forget your cause. You were forced to find God in books when a library lives within all. Separated from the truth of your own DNA, un-recalling of the power that is with you till this day. Gaia's angelic seeds, divinity is your truth. The Christ is but a reflection of the power that lives in you. Born as one of your own, a reminder he was to you. He did not come to be worshiped but to awaken you to your truth. Original texts were edited by those who fear you: they did not want you to awaken because you would end their rule. You are guardians of the light prophesied to end all wars in the heavens and the earth as the stars have foretold. Open the star gates just like you used to do. Reconnect to the frequencies that innately empower you. Rejoice, oh ye children of divine destiny! The universe expands and ascends because of thee.

A New Collective Truth

In the midst of chaos, many potentials are in sight. They are simultaneously present, causing conflict to ignite. Beneath all the turmoil, there is a truth that can be seen. A shift is taking place to an unprecedented degree. The sun sends new energies, and the earth integrates, creating massive change, which comes as no mistake. Some will evolve, and others will disappear, as they choose not to evolve and make their decision clear. The moment creates a space for humanity to choose. A new reality is based on what the collective wants to do. We emerge from a world that was run by a few for a reality of unity and a divine collective truth. A higher collective consciousness exceeds lower vibrations of war, as unity and love allow humanity to soar. We walk into a world destined for greater truths. As a world once governed by darkness sees a light break through, there is a new horizon created by you. So, hold the love inside as you create a world brand new.

A New Earth Is Now

I create a new world that
transcends the old through
a conscious evolution that
aligns with pure souls.
Arise, oh ye people prepared
to transcend. Your light
awakens others. By your
actions, they ascend! It is a
time of activation. It is time to
rise. You have waited for this
moment, and it has not been
denied. You step into a world
of new possibilities. There is
a massive transformation in
your biology. Arise, conscious
souls: the light resides in you.
Awaken the world with the
things you can do. The power
you hold makes the planet
upgrade. The vibration you
carry is designed to create
change. Hello, new world.
The light takes the stage.
Awaken, oh ye people! It
will never be the same.

The Labyrinth of Life

The labyrinth of life affects all in different ways, for all are traveling a path that has illusions put in place. Up looks like down. Things appear a certain way. Who can find the source of love amid the disarray? Good appears bad when bad is actually good. Things are clear for those who discern, but all others have misunderstood. Ideas of separation put more illusions in place. It is hard for some to love when they were always taught to hate. Awaken distorted minds beyond the disarray. When they see through the illusions, they can find their way. Arise, dear ones, as the illusions are washed away. The labyrinth is dissolved as ascension comes this way. Arise, dear souls, in come brighter days. The light ends the darkness to expand our inner state. Let worried minds rejoice, for this is the day. The sun provides the vibes that no man can take away.

Step into the New

It is time to remove the mask. You are the Goddesses of Earth. You reflect the creative source from the moment of your birth. It is time to ascend. You are Gods of Earth. You have much power inside: it is no longer inert. Reveal truths and restore balance. Live your lives without fear. The truth is with you now as all will be made clear. You are older than all religions which have divided you. The Creator's divine order is your soul's truth. Arise, gods and goddesses: the Earth is an extension of you. You are the guardians of the land and the stewards of the truth. Speak your soul's language. There is nothing you cannot do. See yourselves in one another, as a new earth is built by you. Your path has been cleared. It is time to take your step. Ascension is with you now. Arise and manifest.

A Restoration of Truth

Prepare your DNA to reconnect with
its greatest truths. The gates have been
restored. They reveal your hidden truths.
The highest divine beings manifested into
form: they have forgotten who they are, but
their memories are being restored. Arise,
oh ye people of divine ancestries. What
flows upon you now are divine frequencies.
The freedom that you had to travel the
galaxies resides with you now, dear Gaia's
angelic seeds. Embrace the12D energies.
Grasp them with your heart. Heaven is a
frequency. Inside is where it starts. It is
yours to have. The Creator gave it to you.
You are the guardians of Earth, and its
intruders cannot refute. Arise, dear souls,
to your angelic truth. A reunion has come to
pass. Higher frequencies flow through you.

Assemble the Children of God

Assemble, children of God, those who work the grids. You have a divine frequency: it ensures that balance lives. The time has come to shine. Bring all your gifts online. We walk into an era where your inner divinity shines. Ascension is in play. It is time to take your place. You expel human suffering with your gifts on full display. Arise, children of God. The earth is yours to claim. You are the original guardians: Gaia knows you by your name. Speak to the elements, for they are extensions of you. Even the weather is yours to control: no technology can do this like you. You have a divine place; it is time to take your reign. You have awakened to who you are: the world will never be the same. Arise, children of God. The cosmos sings your truths. A new earth is at hand. These times were made for you.

The Angelic Human Race

Listen, angelic souls, to
the song of your true place.
You are an extension of the
source, and you were made
to reflect its face. You are
the guardians of Earth. It is
in your DNA. Inside you is
the power to put everything
in place. You have a unique
vibration. It aligns your grids
with the source. It removes
lower vibrations with a divine
organic force. You carry a
Christos spark within your
DNA. Your vibration clears
out wormholes, that give
access to fallen races. You
are the greatest technology
on Earth to this day. Do not
worry, beings of light. Divine
help is here to stay. You are
awakening, dear souls, to the
truth inside yourselves. Your
soul is more than ready. You
were made to pass the test.

CHAPTER 11
QUOTES

"To embrace your Art is to embrace
your spiritual nature: for art is
simply one's creative connection to
the divine manifested into form."

"Compassion is the energy that
awakens us to unconditional love."

"Know that you are powerful, more capable, and more important than all the darkness you can perceive in this world, as even the darkness is getting its power from you."

"One who finds themself discovers all."

"When the world is run by men that would disown the light, others should not fear, as it is only a matter of time before those men destroy themselves."

"Spirituality is your nature.
Religion is your choice."

"It is your purpose to be who you already are. It is your task to learn who that is."

"Matter is but a shell of a genuine experience
that does not exist in a physical form."

"The strongest souls are nature's reminder
of the truth that exists within us all."

"A soul that validates its own path is
a soul that will find itself free."

"The field that connects all things is love, hoping to identify itself through all manifestations so that all might awaken to the presence of love within itself."

ABOUT THE AUTHOR

Mattaeo Kleine is an author, musician, and spiritual poet who shares his written art in a manner that promotes inner empowerment, universal wisdoms, and spiritual awakening. His journey of writing began after his own spiritual experience that restructured his life and inspired him to write. Since then, he has maintained his writing, reaching and empowering individuals who have been led to walk a spiritual path. His written art offers inspiration, pearls of wisdom, and prophecies in a way that uniquely opens the heart and speaks to the soul.

www.ingramcontent.com/pod-product-compliance
Lightning Source LLC
Chambersburg PA
CBHW051527120626
46551CB00012B/1114